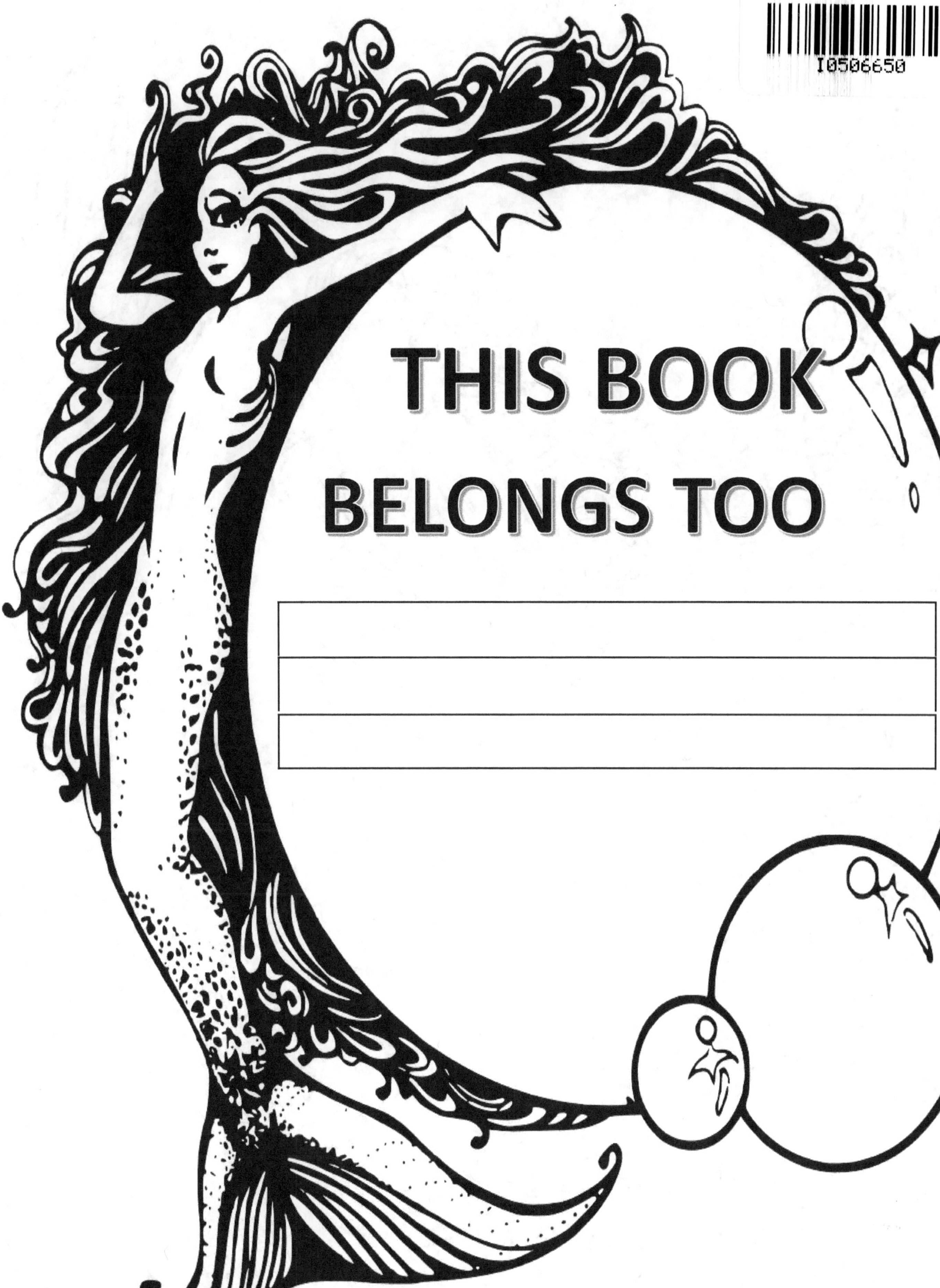
THIS BOOK
BELONGS TOO

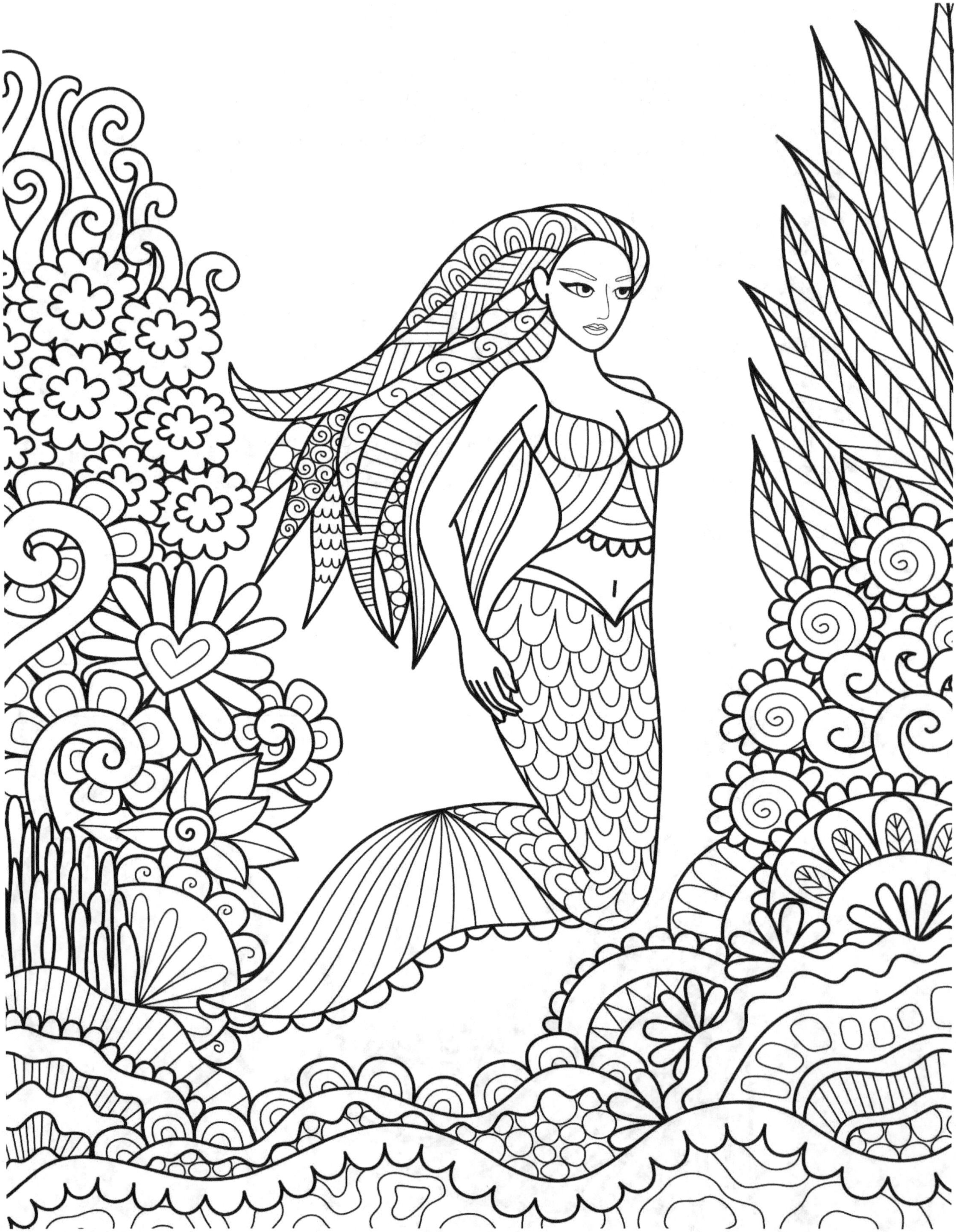

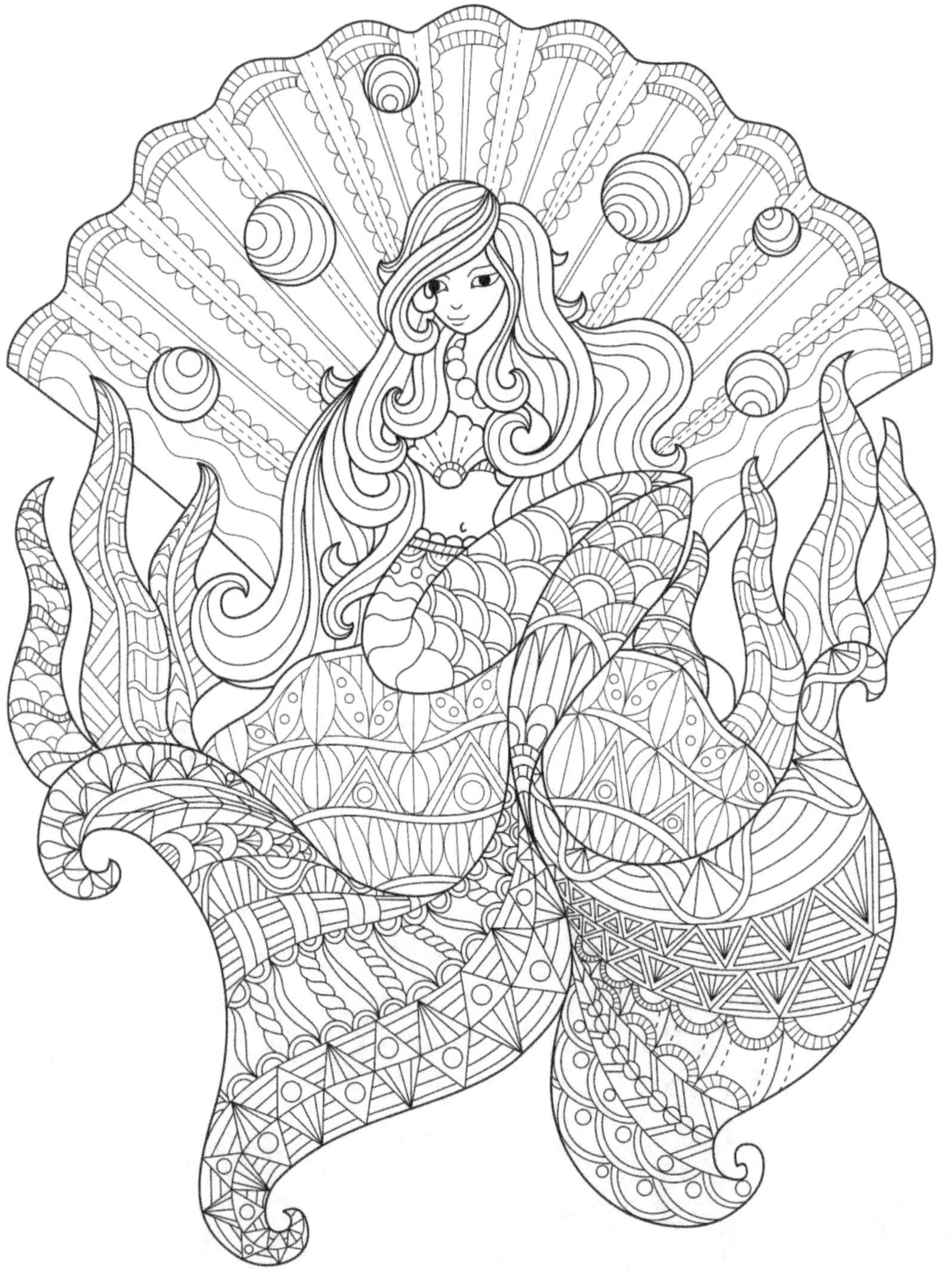

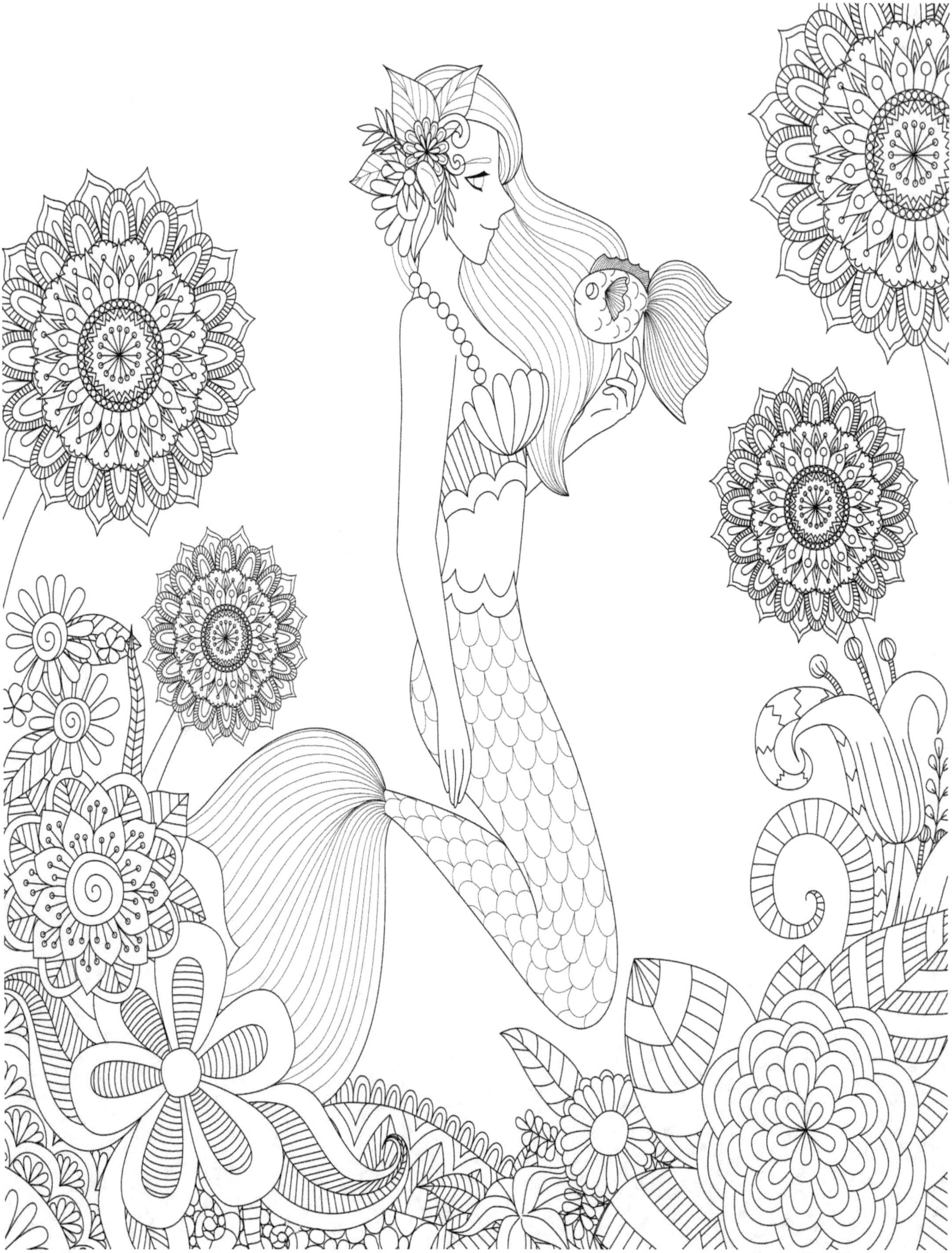

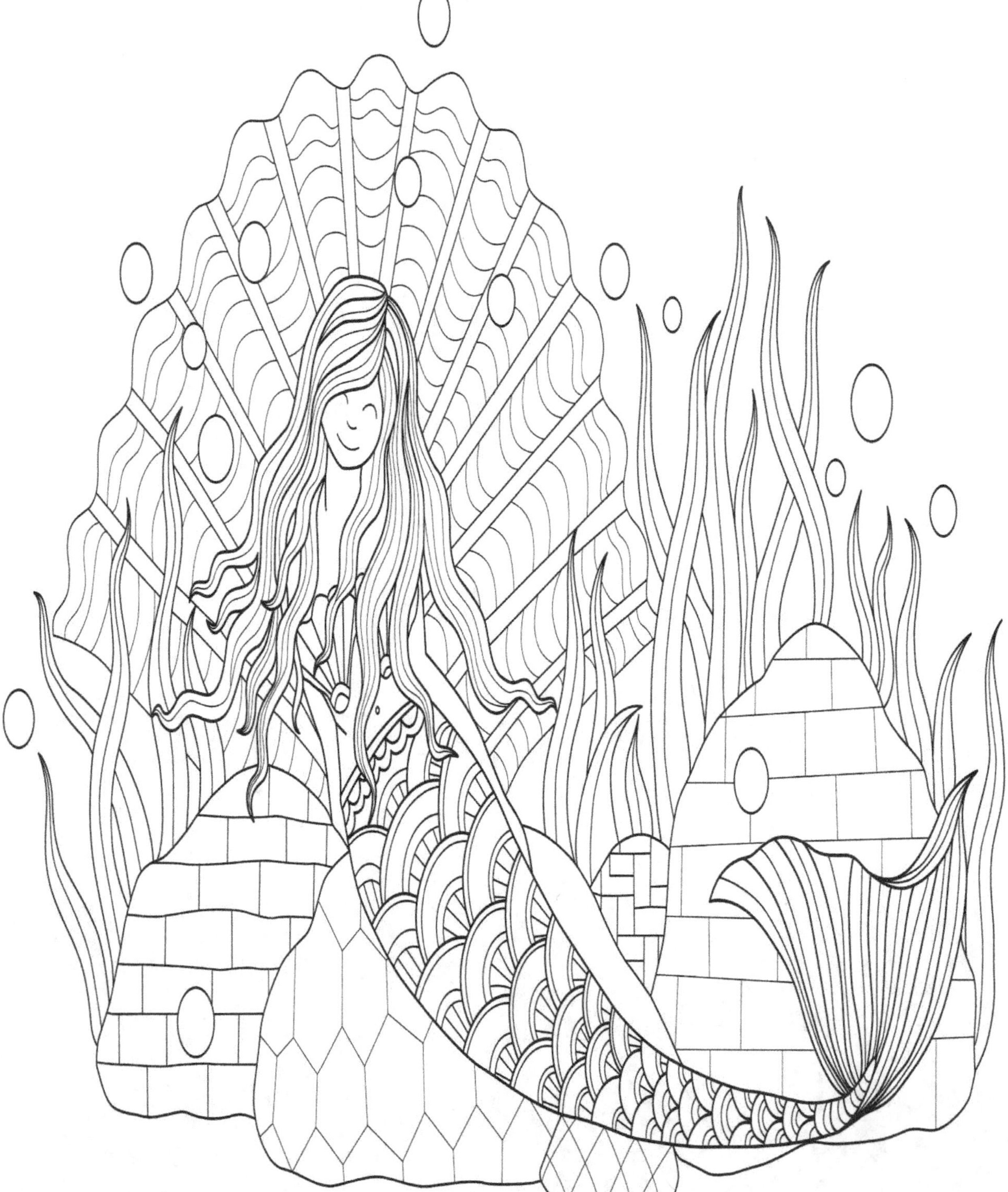

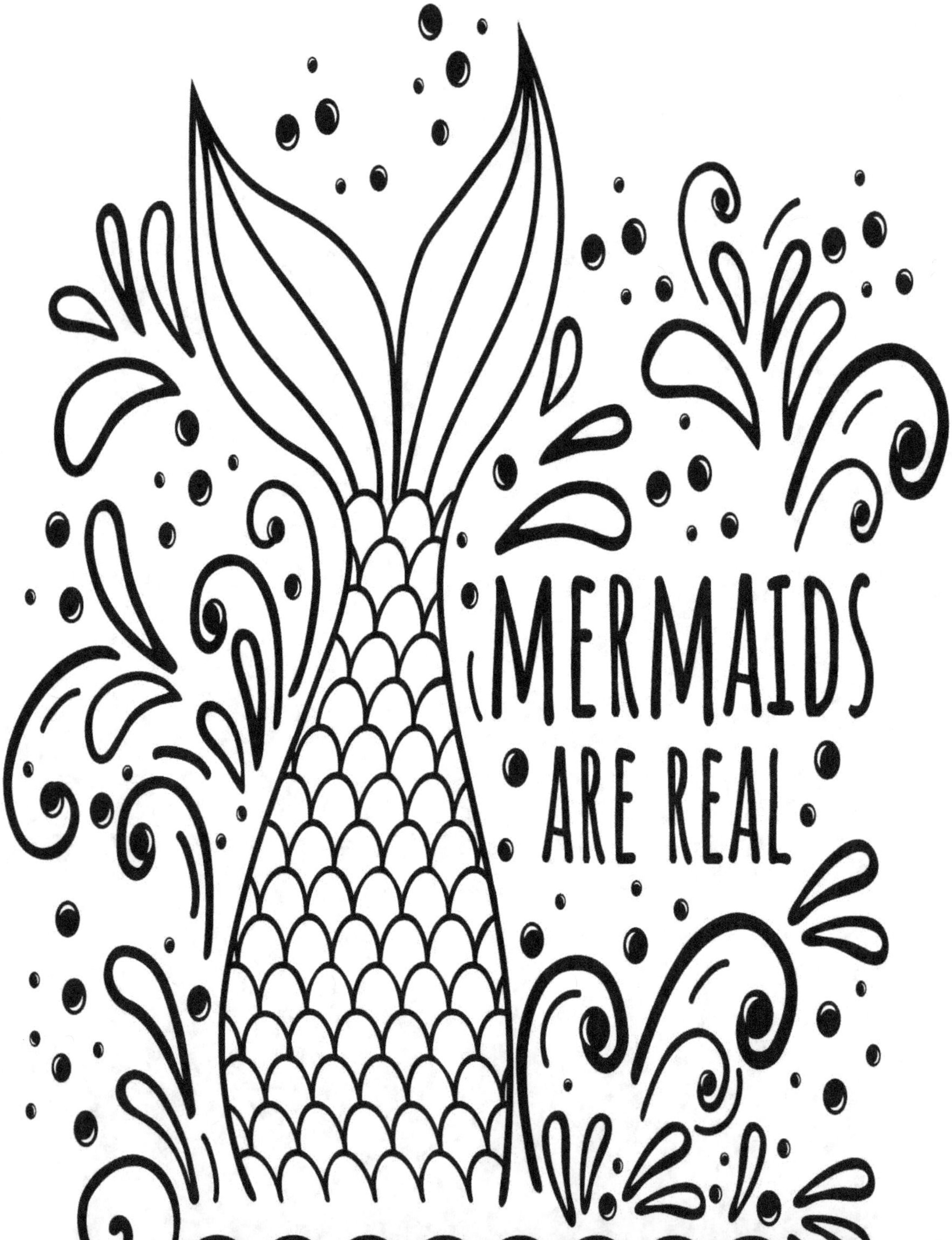
MERMAIDS
ARE REAL

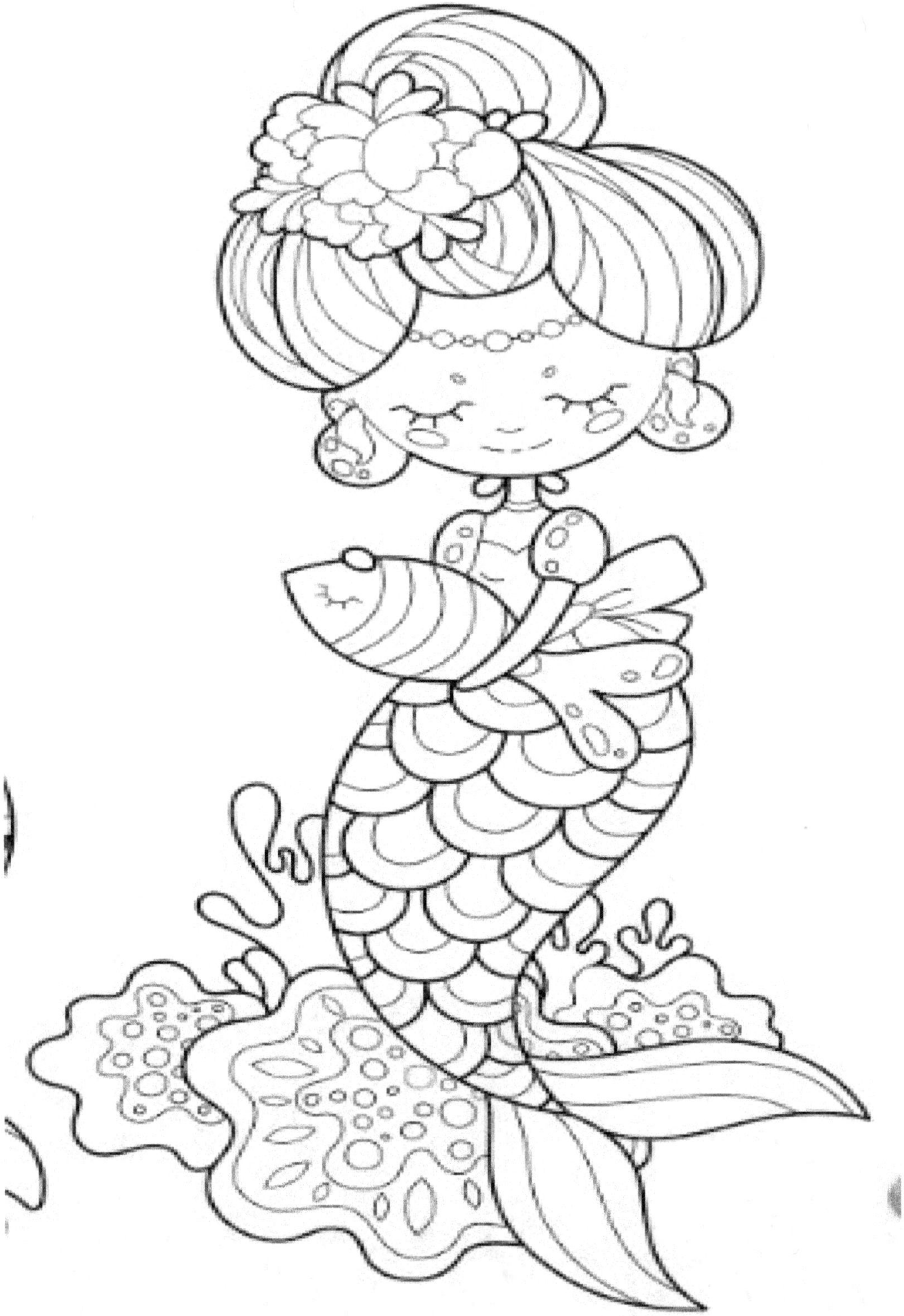

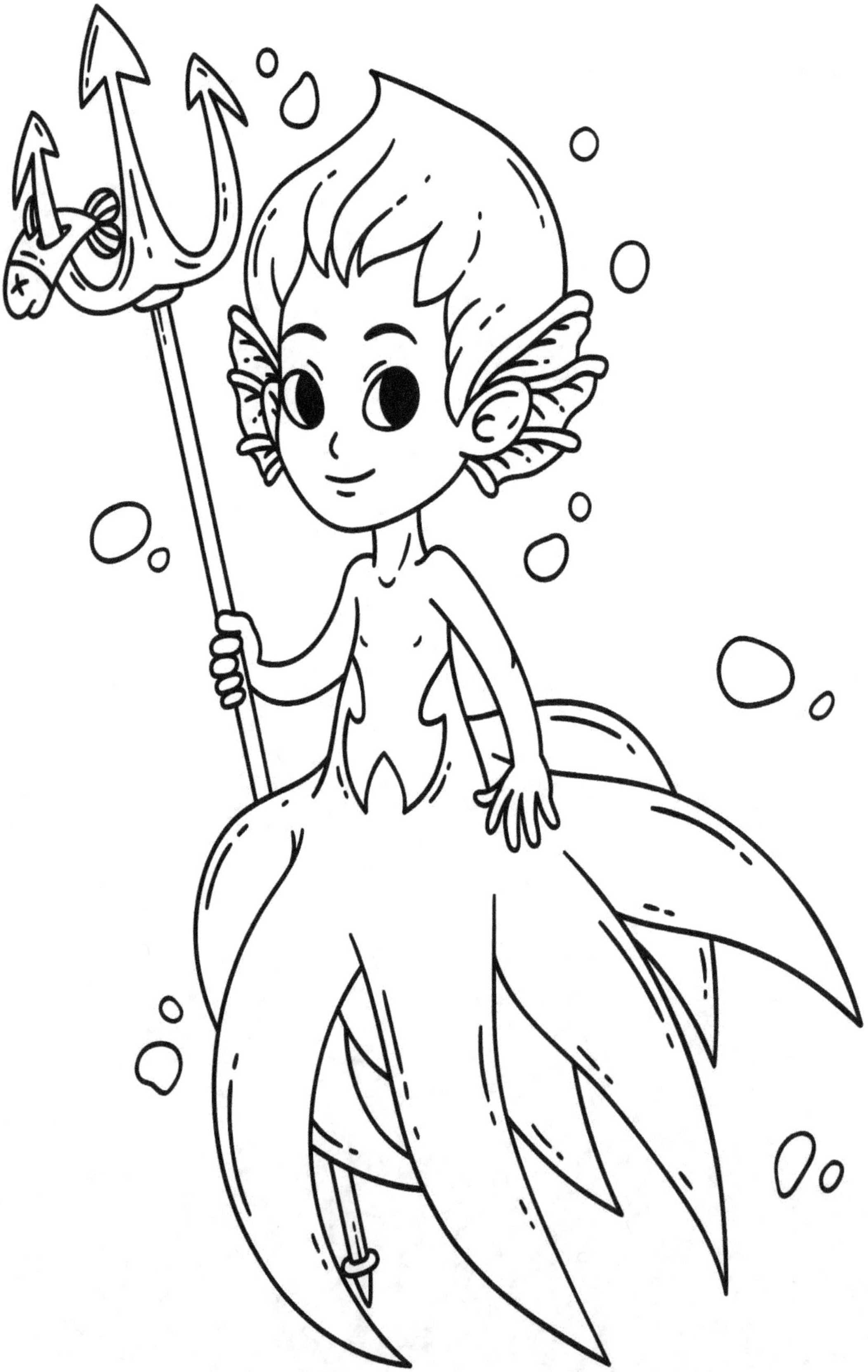

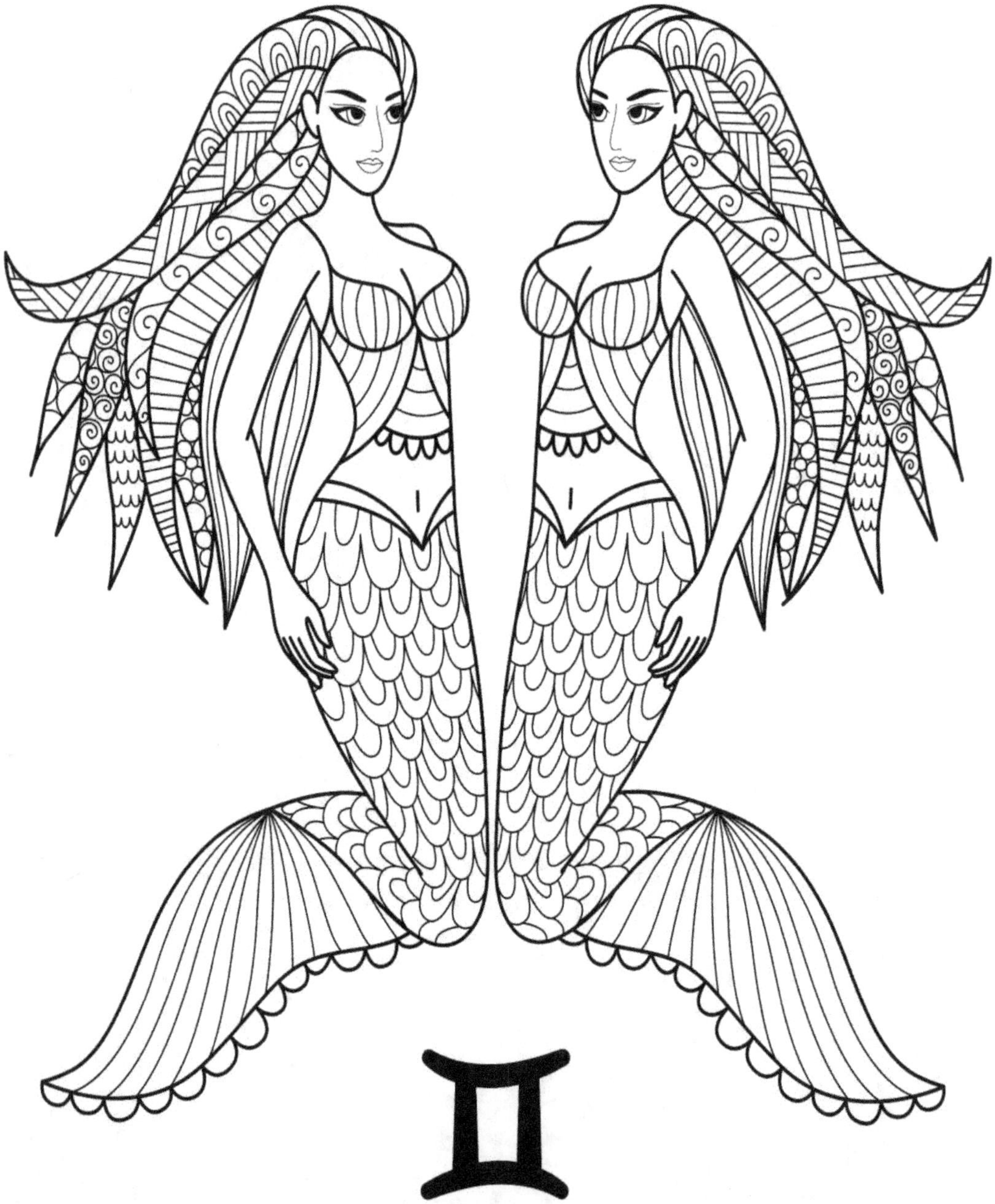

GEMINI

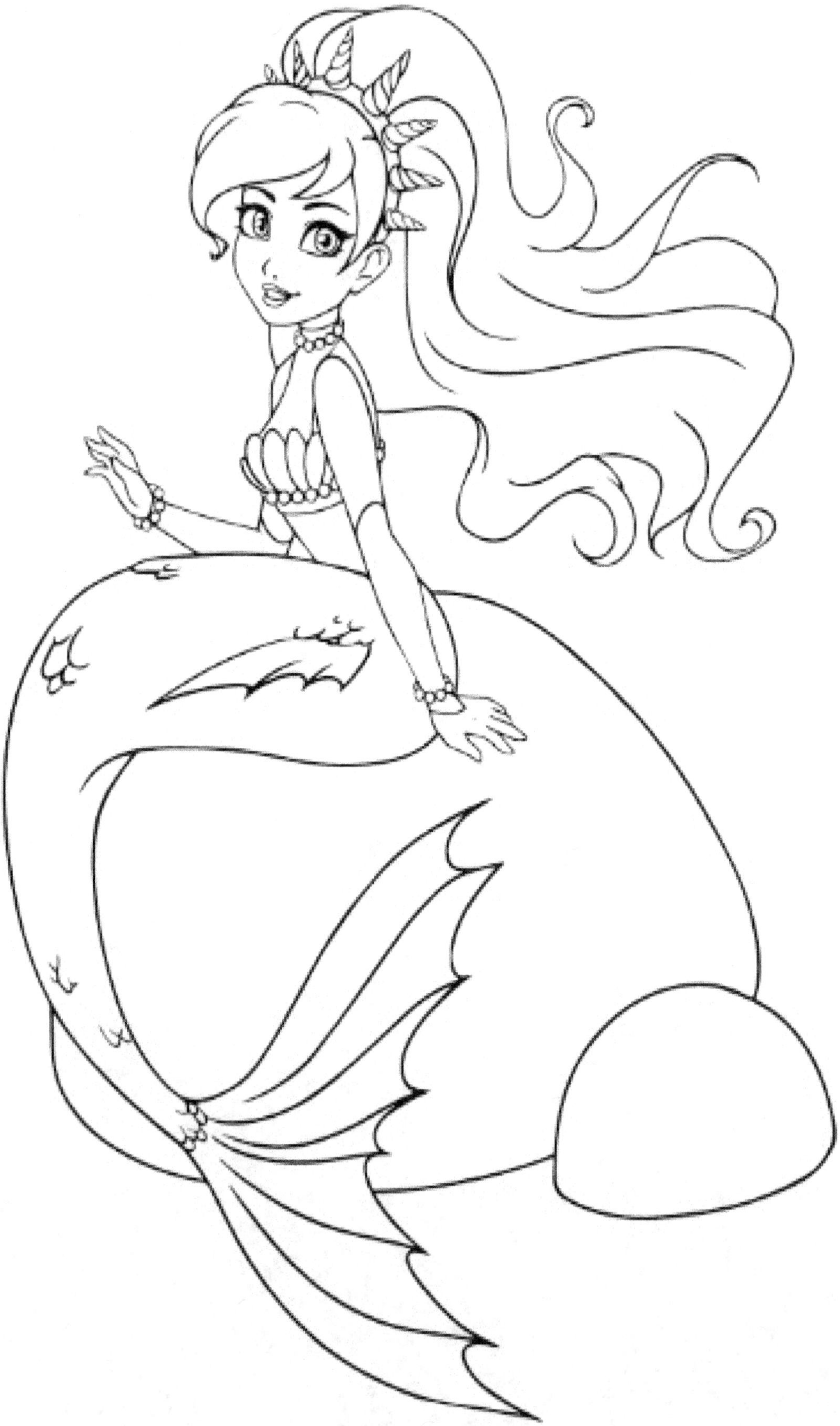

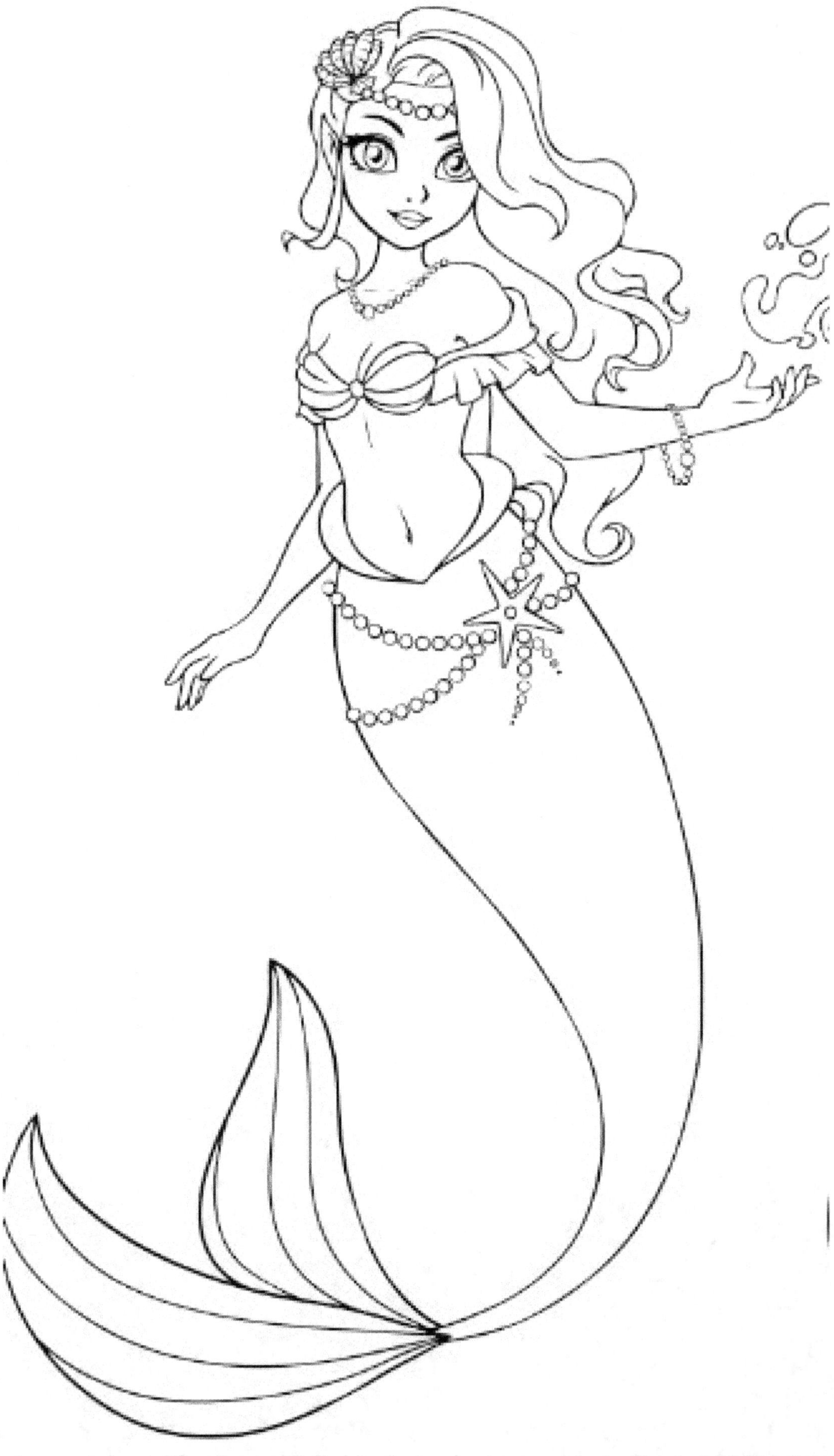

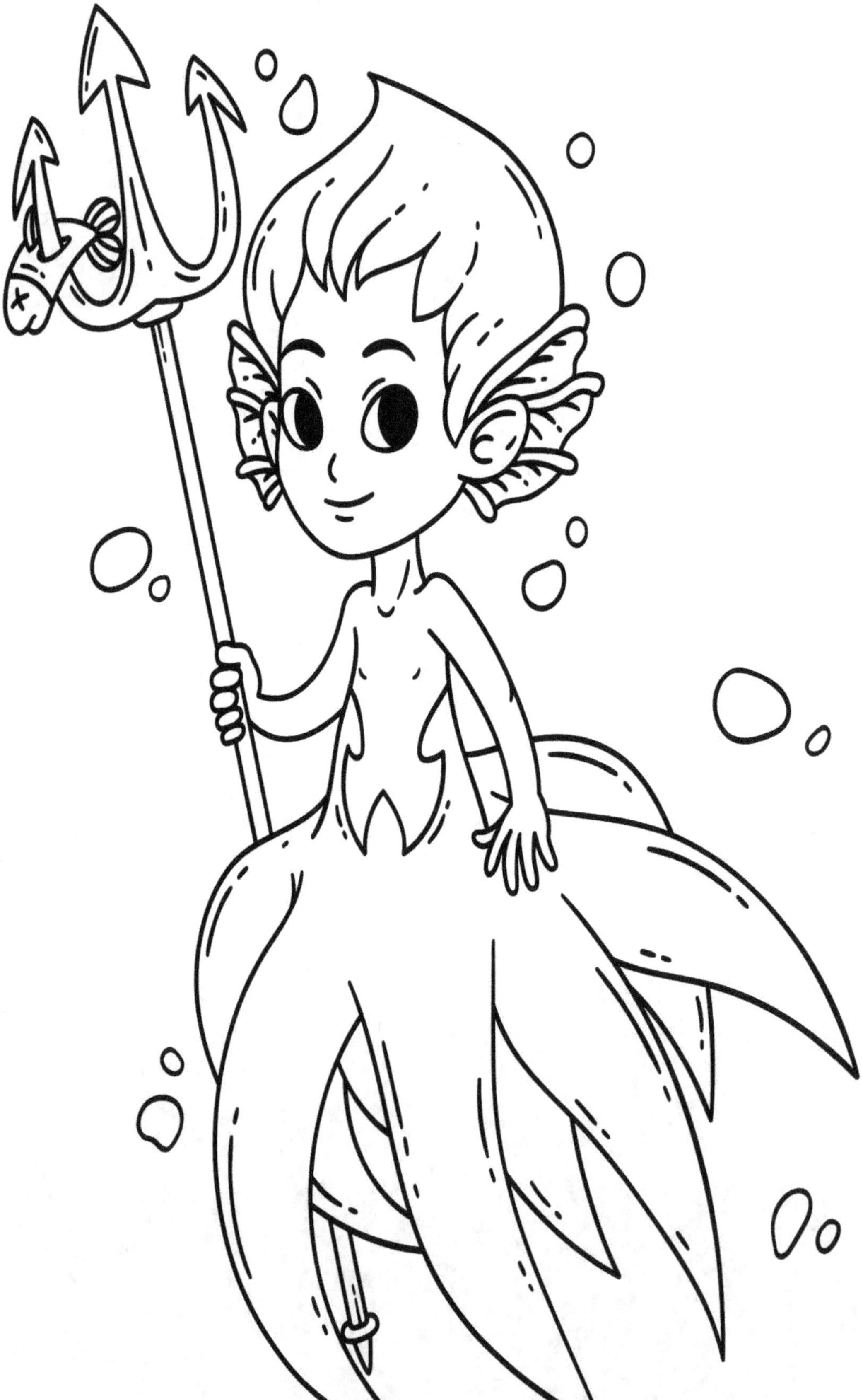

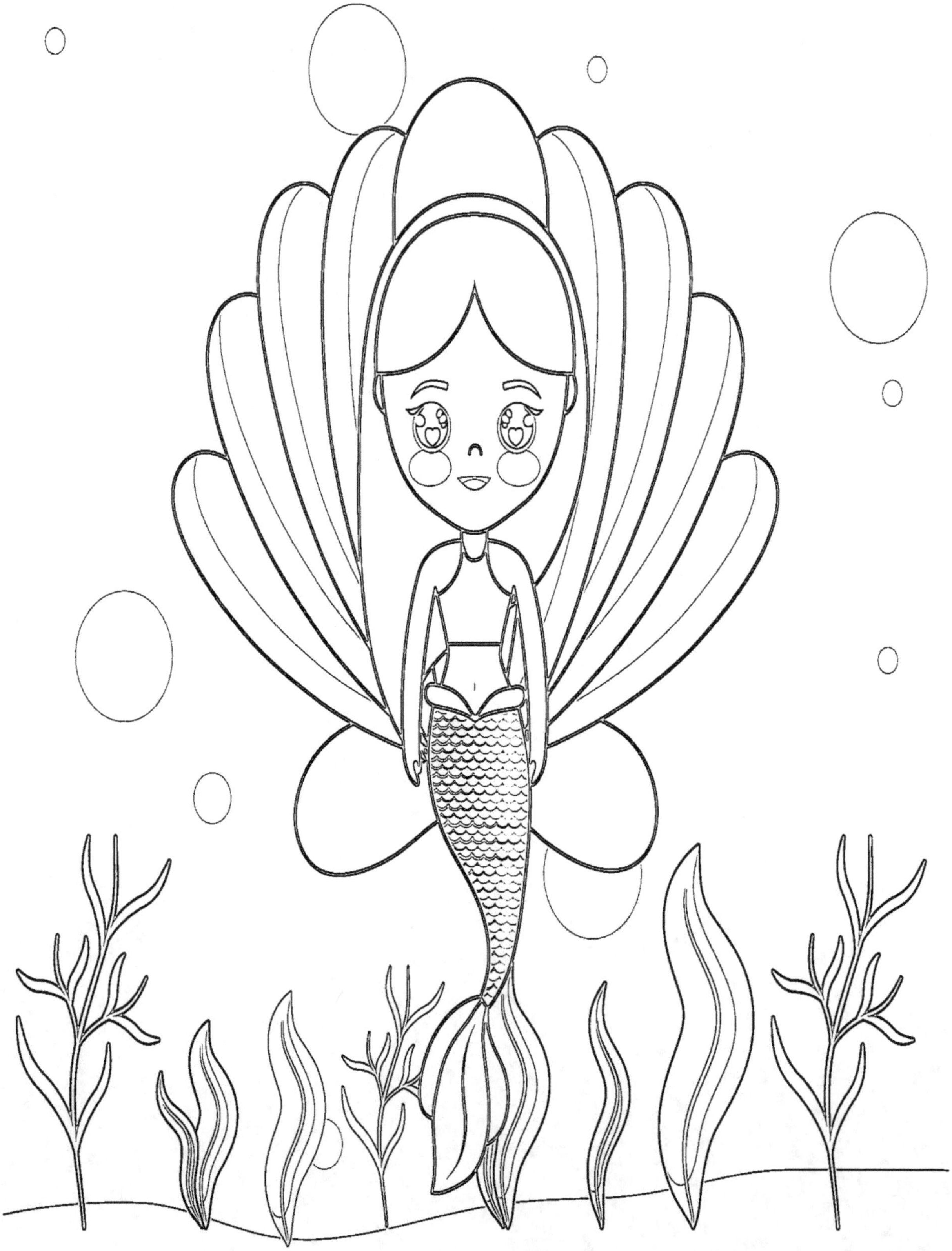

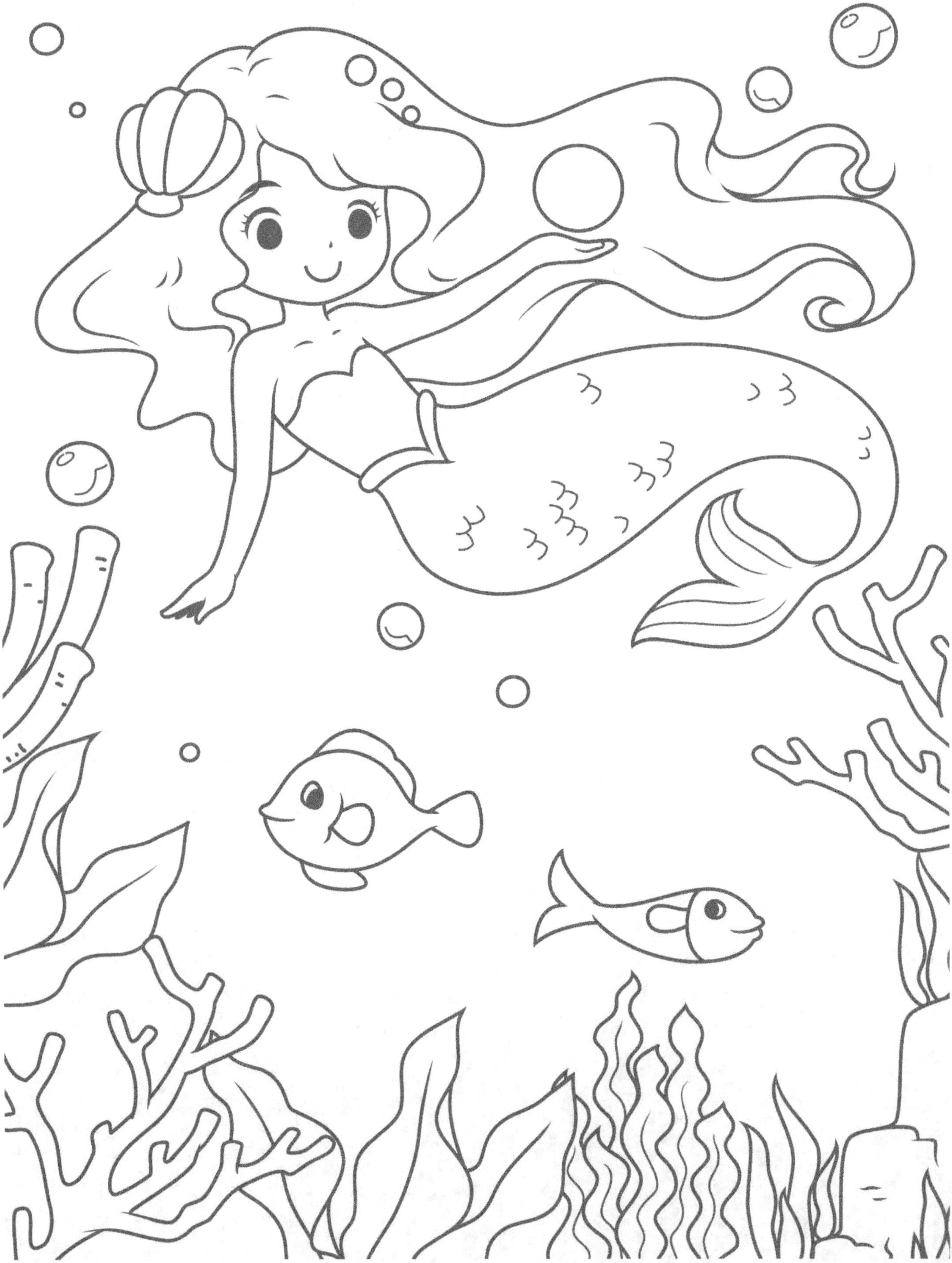

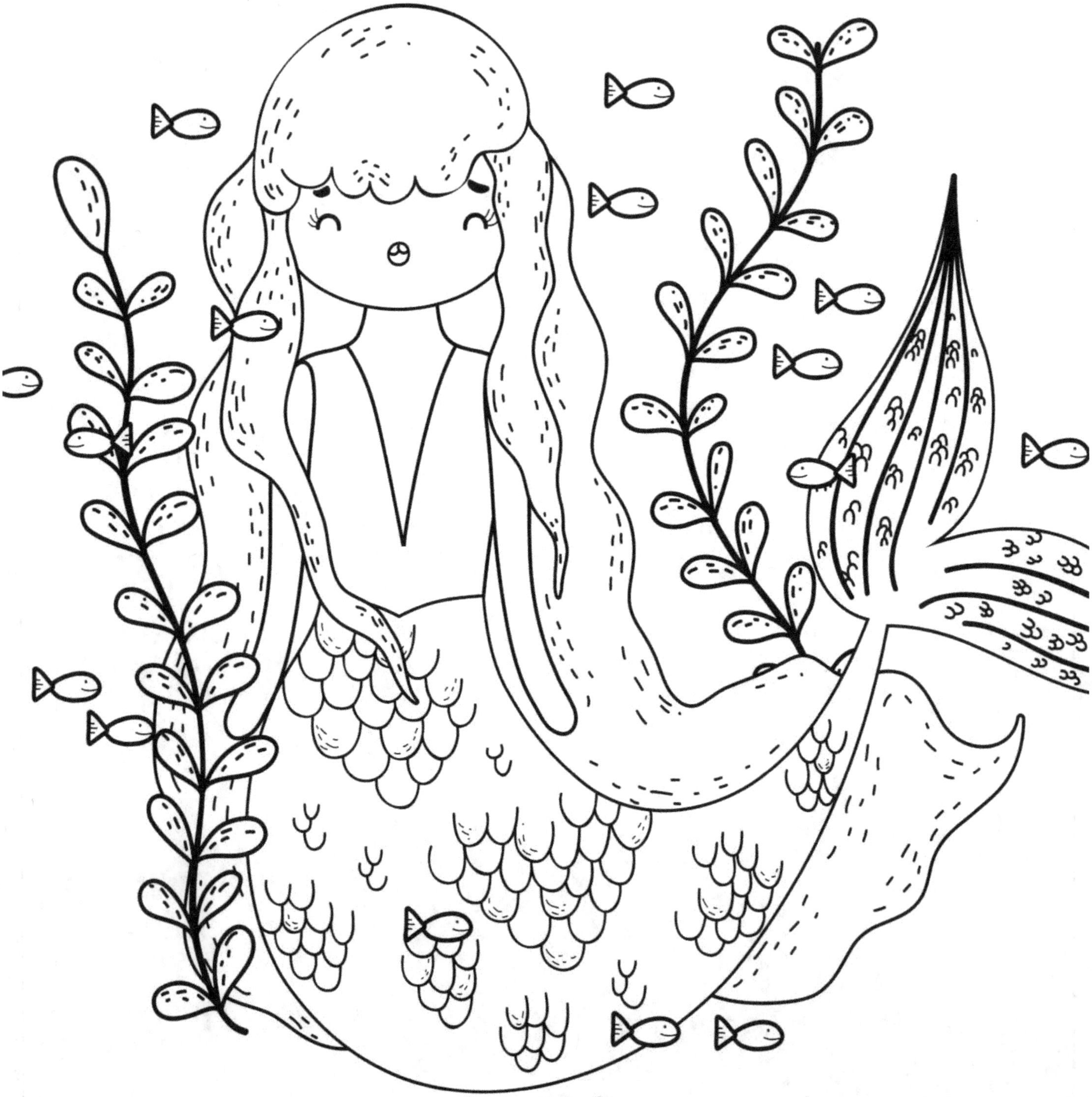

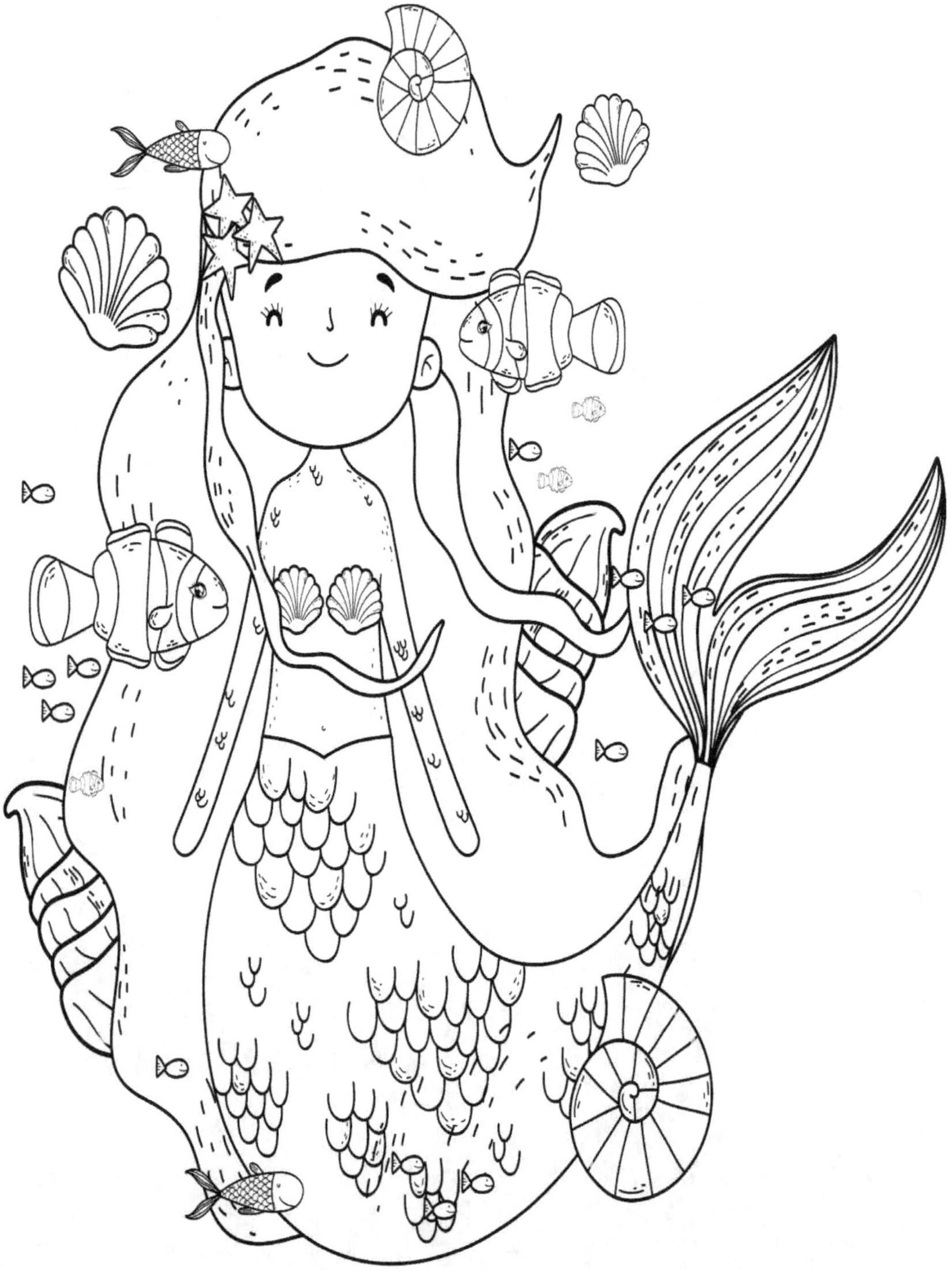

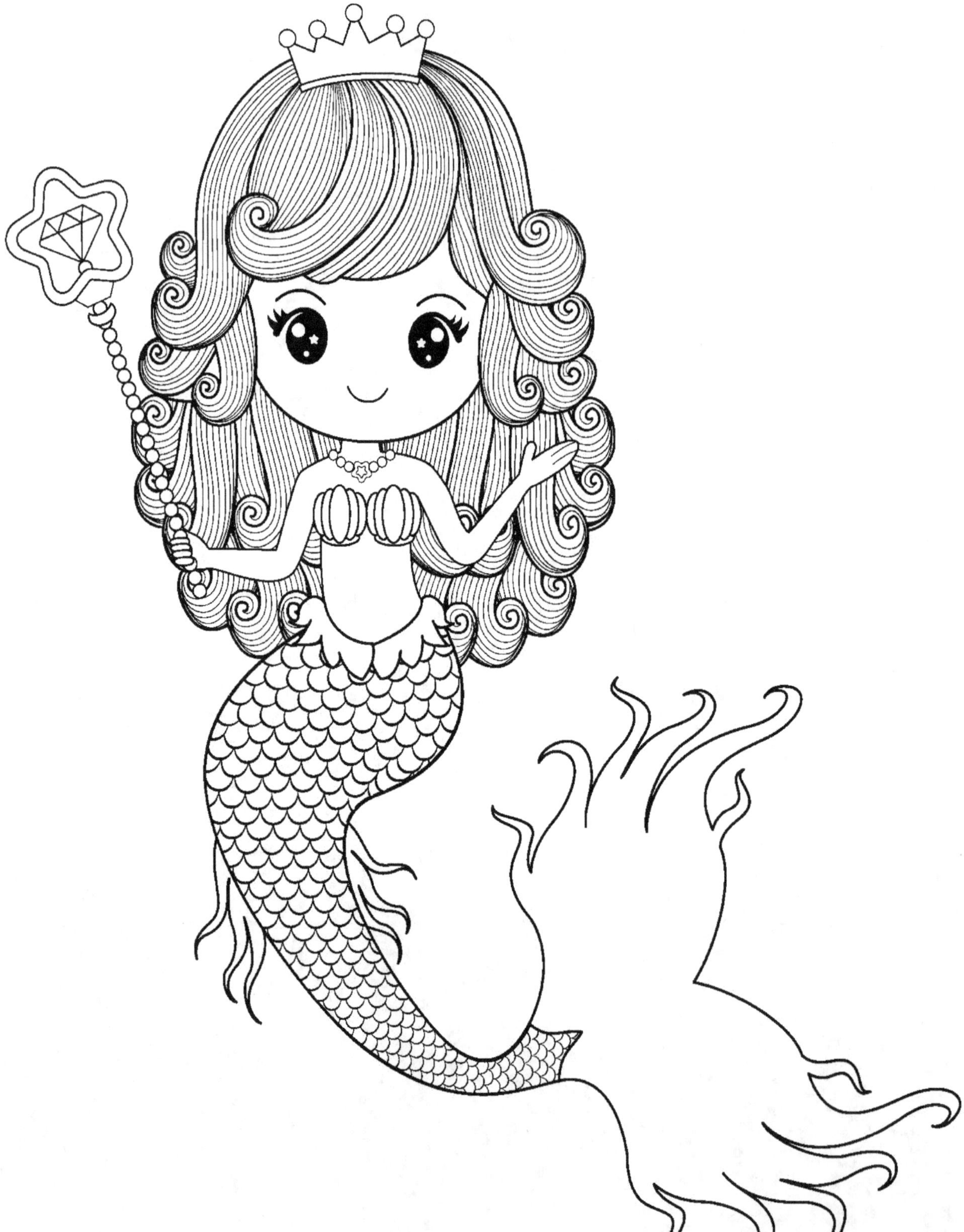

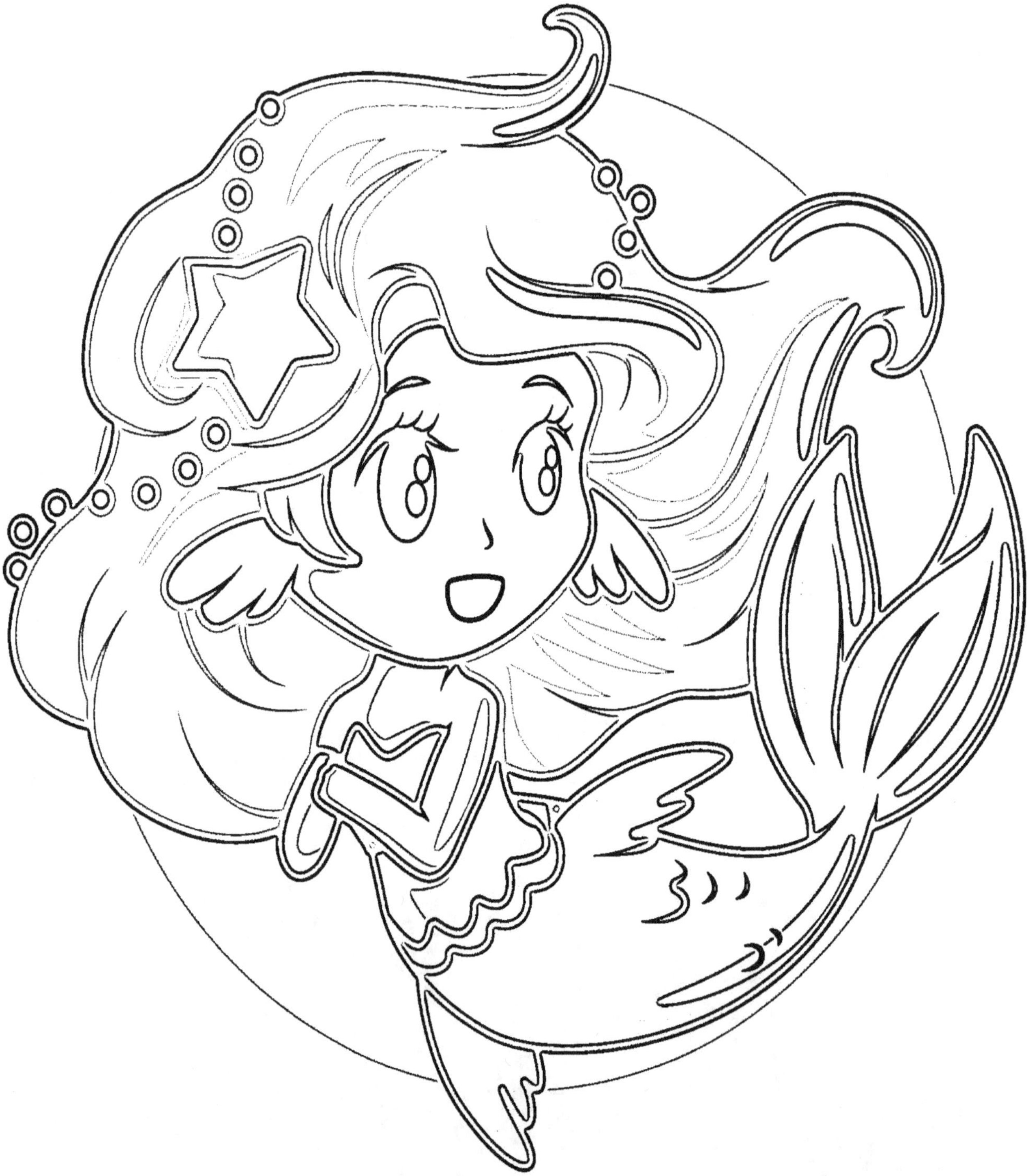

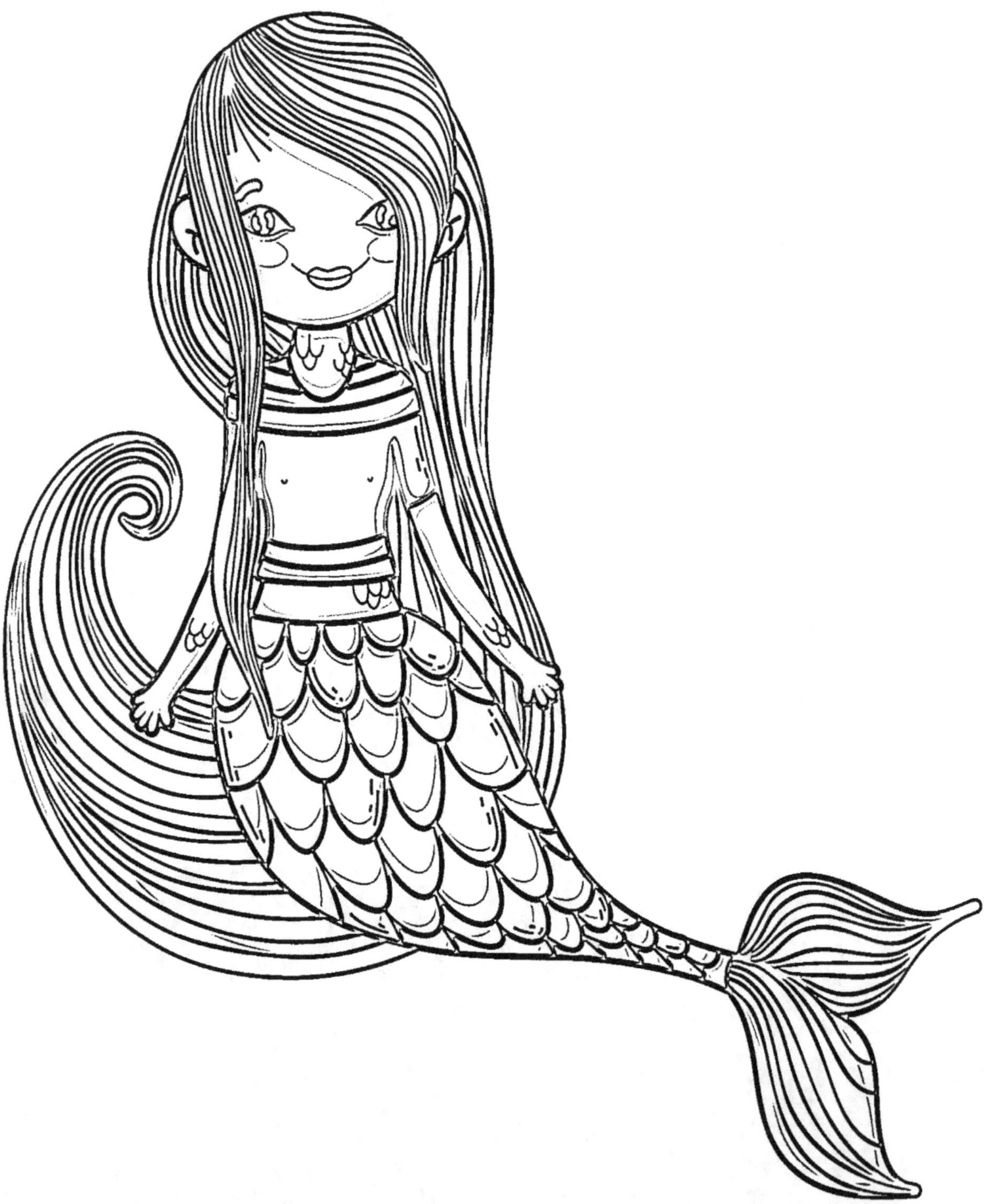

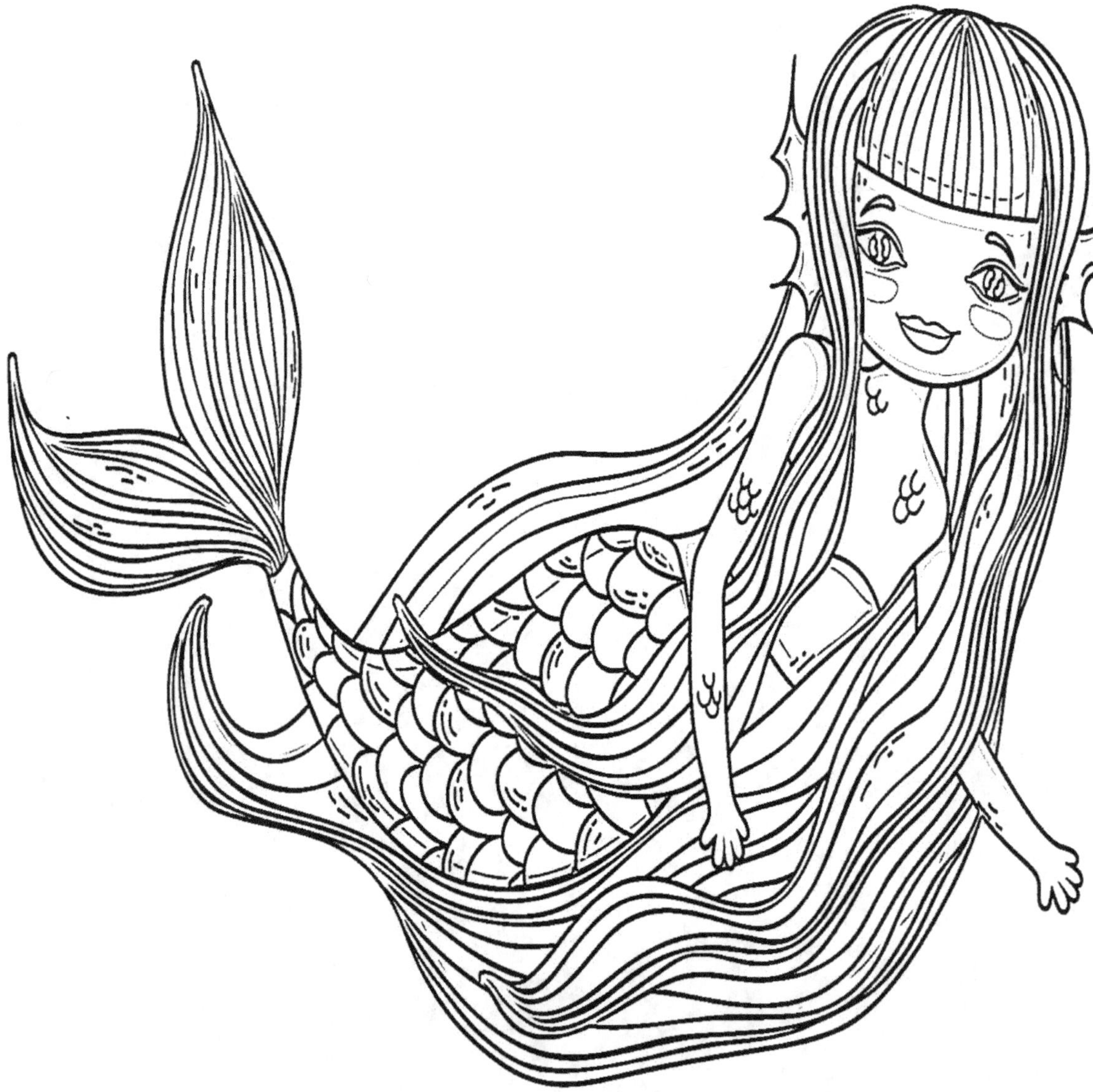

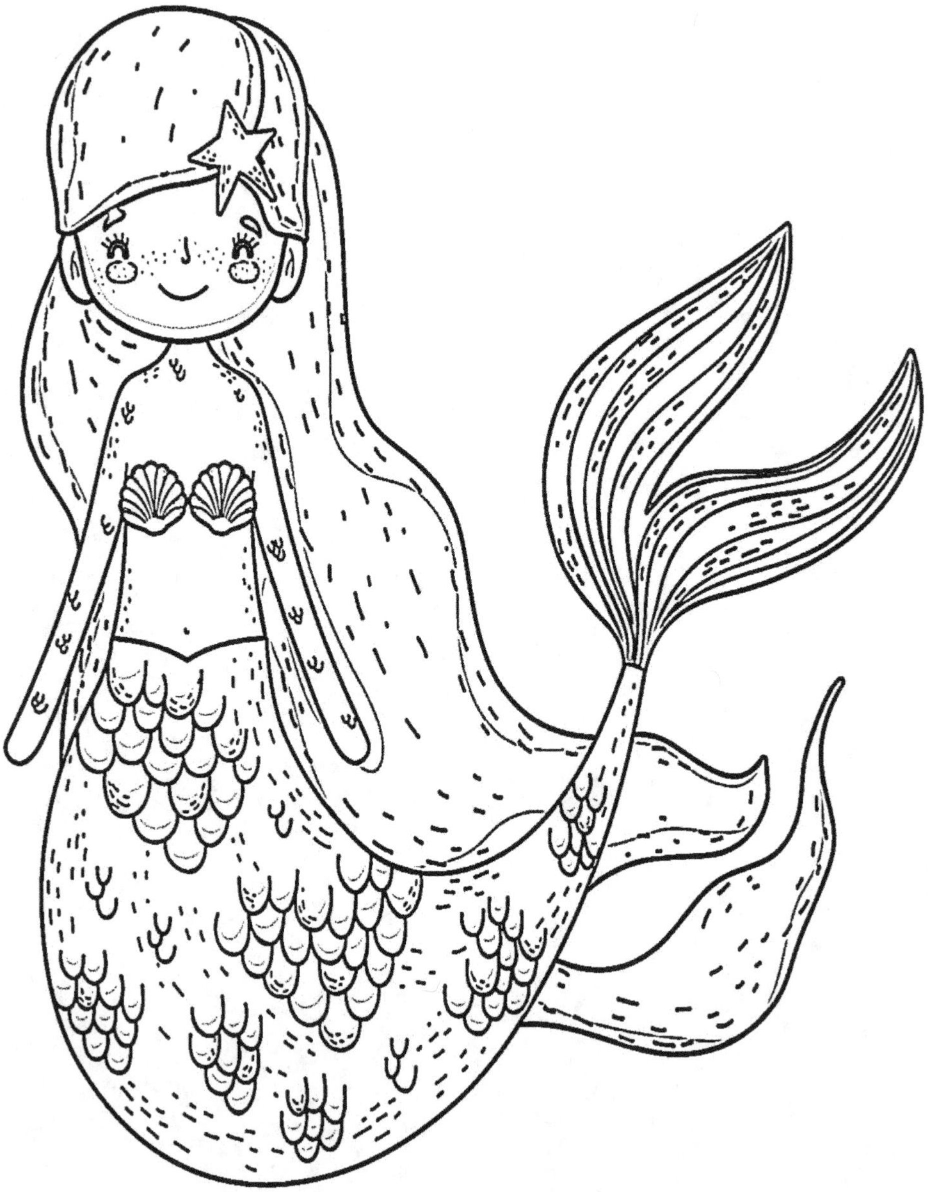

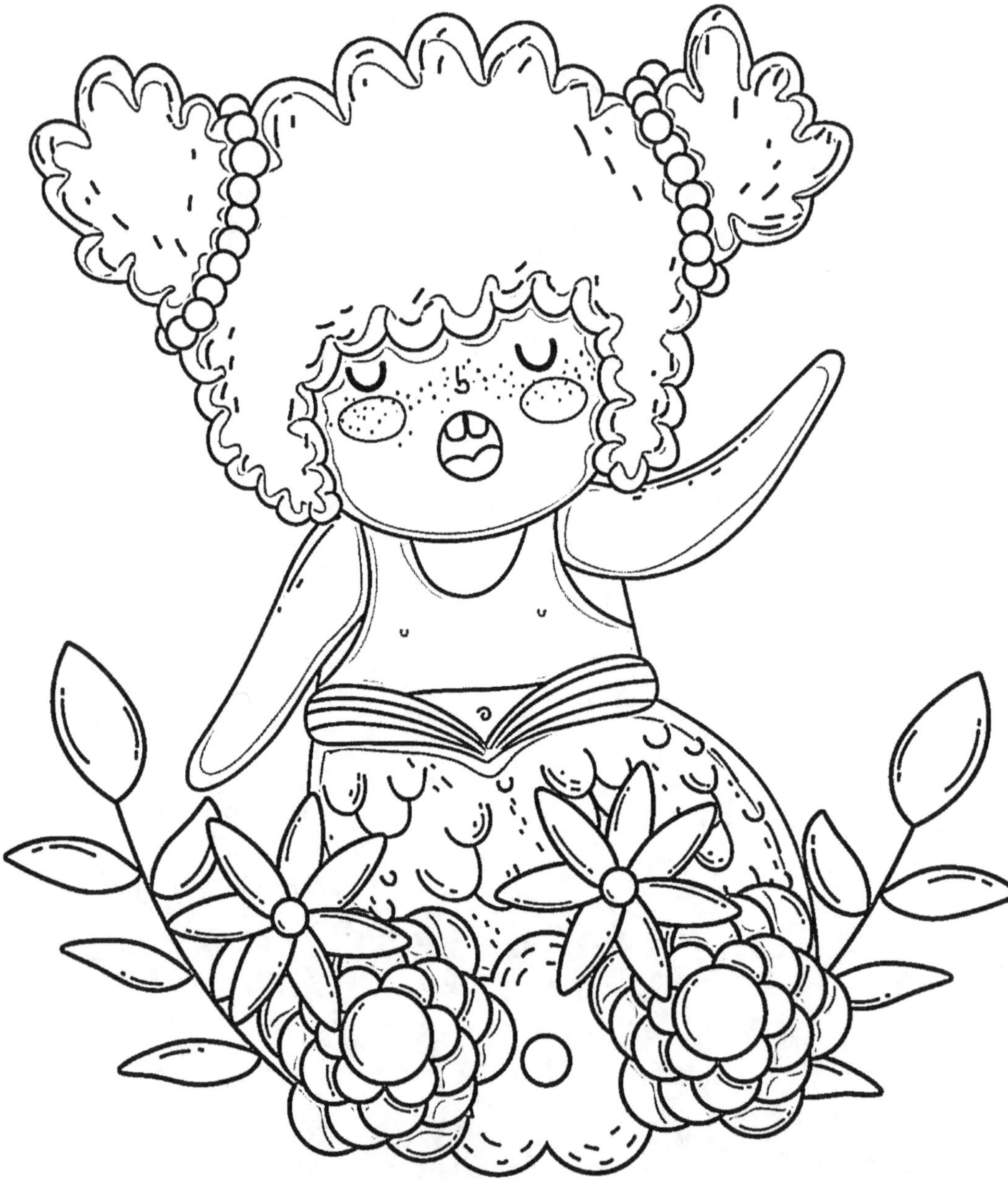

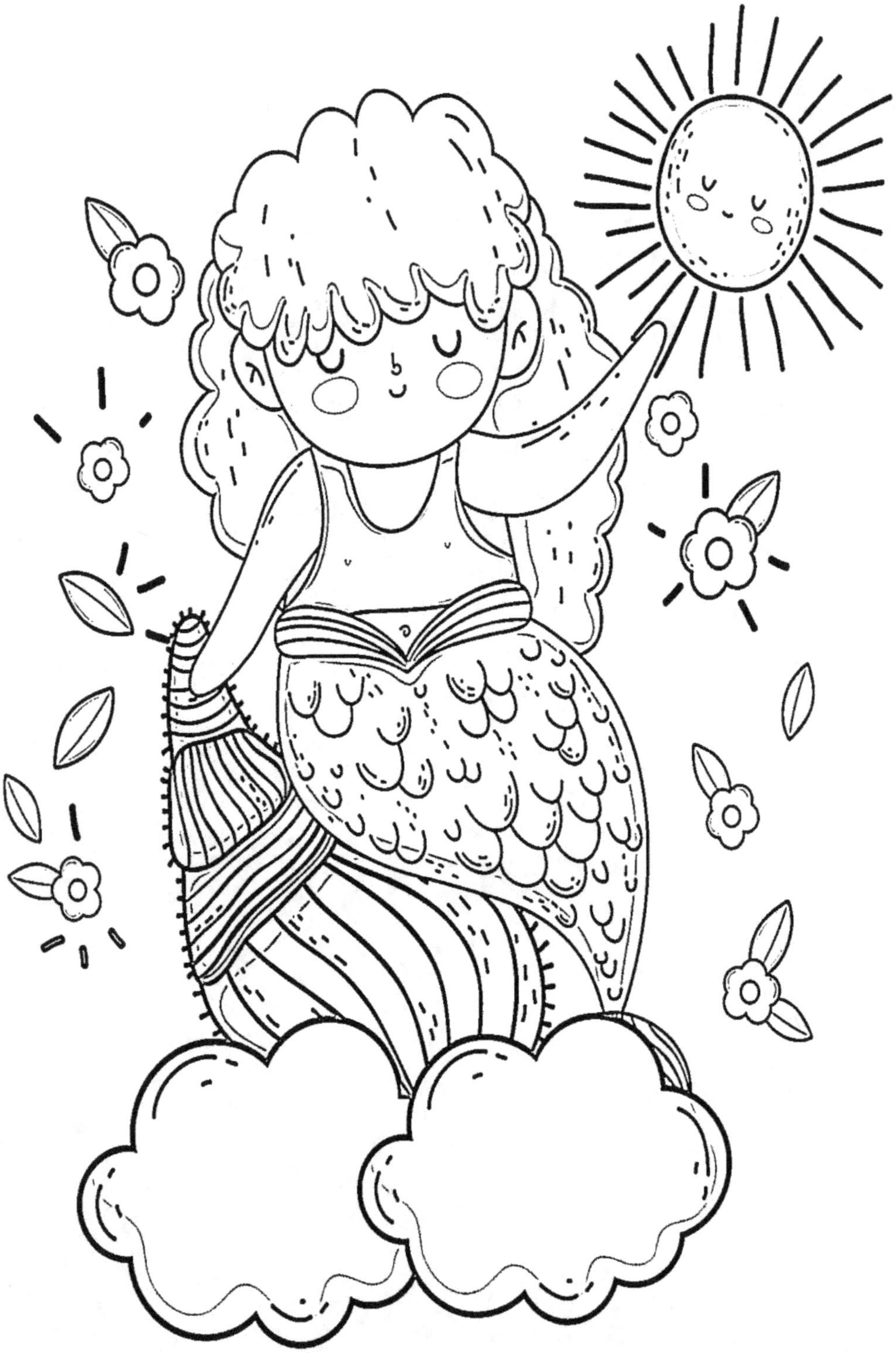

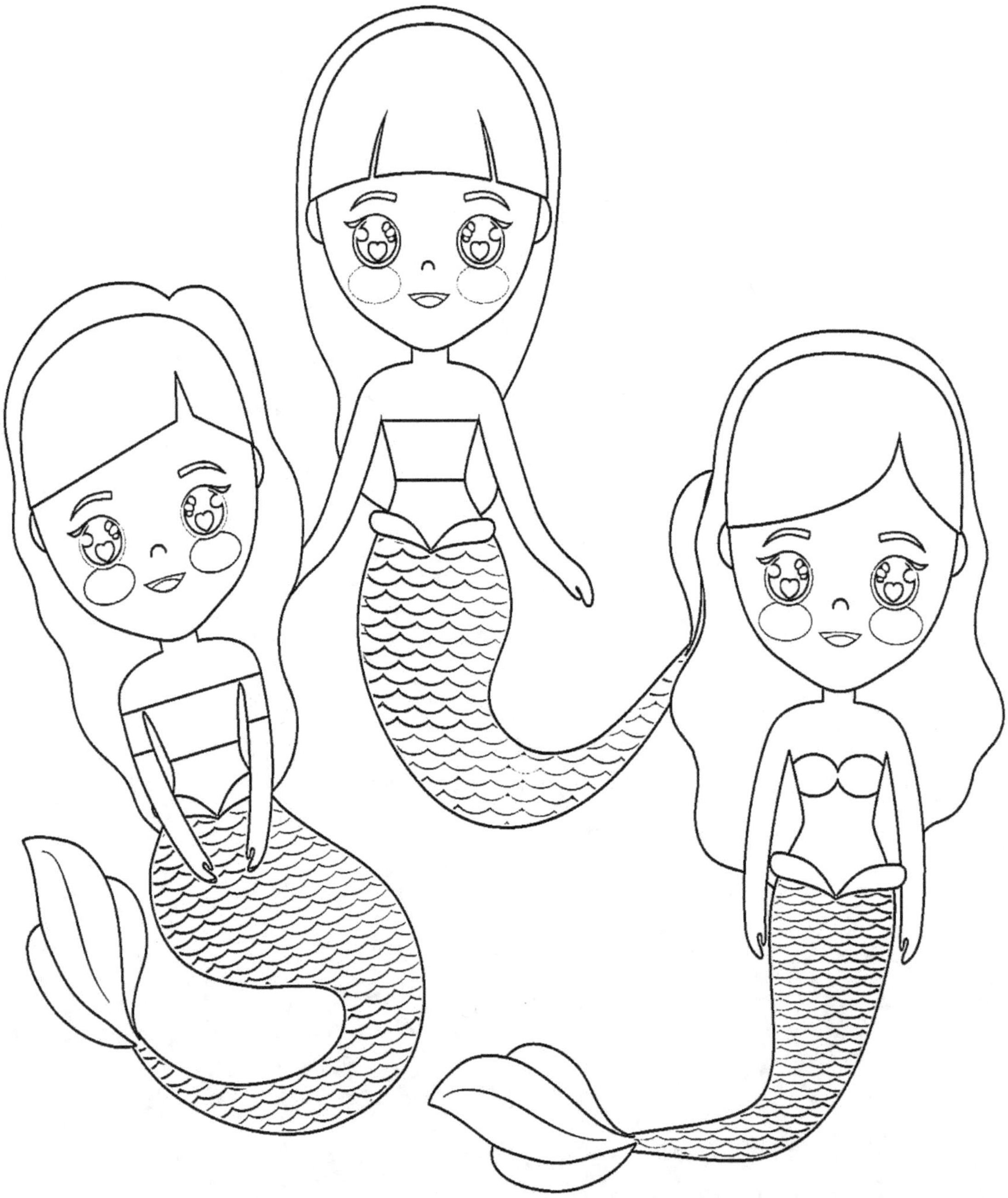

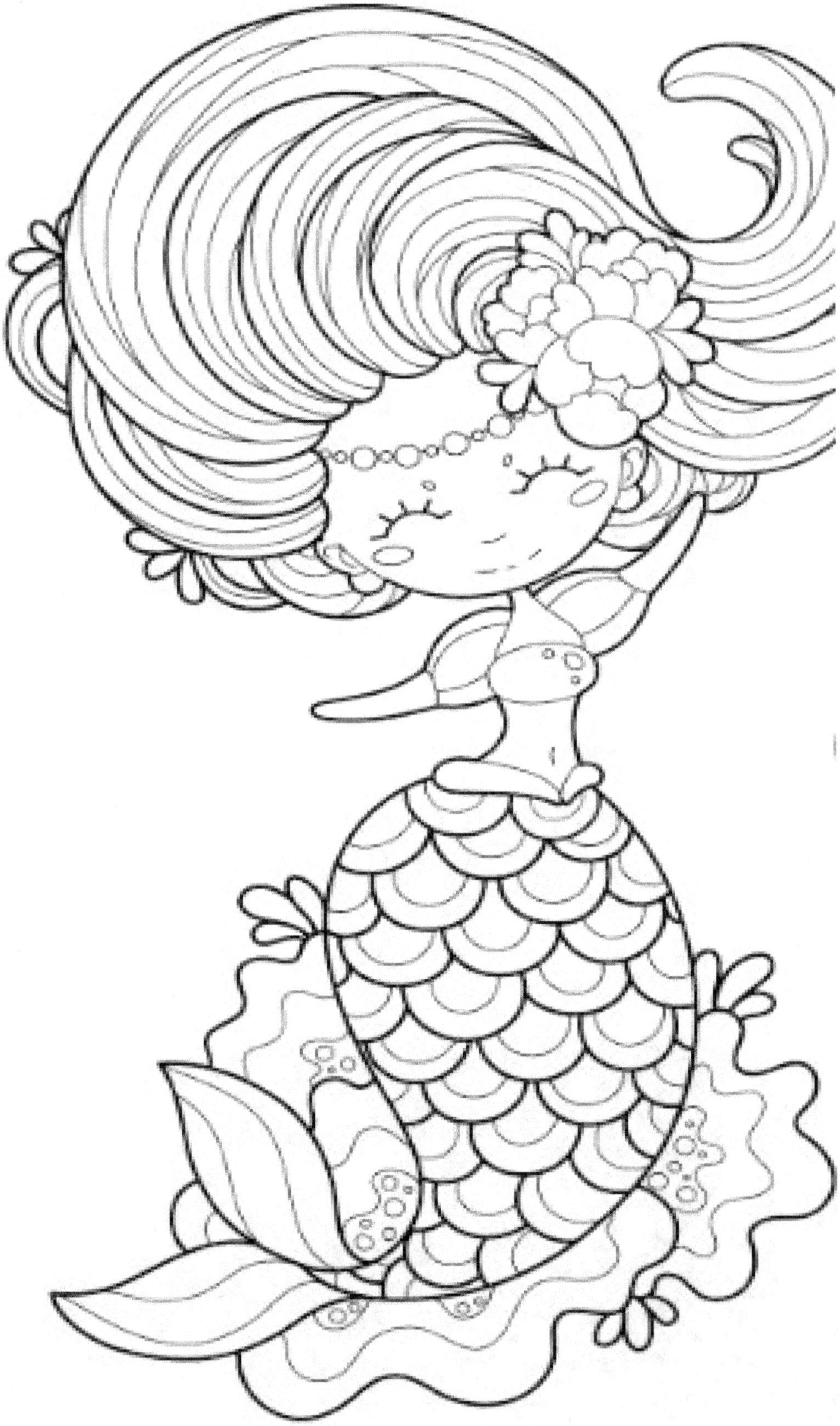

NOTE

www.ingramcontent.com/pod-product-compliance
Lightning Source LLC
Chambersburg PA
CBHW080955220526
45465CB00008BA/3297